MW01202273

The BUCKSKIN MARE

written by Baxter Black   illustrated by Dave Holl

COYOTE C_____ _MPANY
RECORD S_____ _PRESS

D_

All poetry written by Baxter Black

Copyright © 1989 by Baxter Black

Published by   Coyote Cowboy Company
                 Record Stockman Press
                 P.O. Box 1209
                 Wheat Ridge, Colorado 80034

LIBRARY OF CONGRESS CATALOGING IN PUBLICATION DATA

Main entry under:
Cowboy Poetry

Bibliography: p
1. Coyote Cowboy Poetry
2. Cowboys–Poetry
3. Poetry–Cowboy
4. Humor–Cowboy
5. Agriculture–Poetic Comment

I.   Black, Baxter, 1945–

Limited Edition Library of Congress Catalog Card Number 89-91964
ISBN 0-939343-05-3

Regular Edition Library of Congress Catalog Card Number 89-91969
ISBN 0-939-343-06-1

OTHER BOOKS BY BAXTER
THE COWBOY AND HIS DOG © 1980
A RIDER, A ROPER AND A HECK'UVA WINDMILL MAN © 1982
ON THE EDGE OF COMMON SENSE, THE BEST SO FAR © 1983
DOC, WHILE YER HERE © 1984
BUCKAROO HISTORY © 1985
COYOTE COWBOY POETRY © 1986
CROUTONS ON A COW PIE © 1988

map

THE BLACKSTONE RANGE

GRASMERE

J=P POINT

SHEEP CREEK

THE DIAMOND A DESERT

SHEEPSHEAD DRAW

HIWAY TO MOUNTAIN HOME

ID
___
NV

BRUNEAU CANYON

YANKEE BILL

N

CALIFORNIA CREEK

DH

RUNNIN' WILD HORSES

The chase, the chase, the race is on
The mustangs in the lead
The cowboys hot behind the band
Like centaurs, blurred with speed
    The horses' necks are ringin' wet
    From keepin' up the pace
    And tears cut tracks into the dust
    Upon the rider's face
        The rank ol' mare sniffs out the trail
        While never breakin' stride
        But fast behind the wranglers come
        Relentless, on they ride
            Until the canyon walls close in
            And punch'em through the gap
            Where bottled up, they paw and watch
            The cowboy shut the trap
                And that's the way it's been out west
                Since Cortez turned'em loose
                We thinned the dinks and with the herd
                We kept an easy truce
                    But someone said they'd all die off
                    If cowboys had their way
                    So they outlawed runnin' horses
                    But who am I to say

'Cause, hell, I'm gettin' older, boys
And though I miss the chase
His time, like mine, has come and gone
We're both so out of place

      The glamour of our way of life
      Belies our common fate
      I'm livin' off my pension check
      And he's a ward of state

            But what a time! When he and I
            Ran hard across the land
            Me breathin' heavy down his neck
            Him wearin' no man's brand

                  No papers gave us ownership
                  To all the ground we trod
                  But it belonged to me and him
                  As sure as there's a God

                        And if I could, I'd wish for him
                        And for myself, likewise
                        To finally cross the great divide
                        Away from pryin' eyes

                              So in the end he has a chance
                              To die with dignity
                              His carcass laid to rest out there
                              Where livin', he ran free

                                    And coyotes chew his moldered bones
                                    A fitting epilogue
                                    Instead of smashed up in a can
                                    For someone's townhouse dog.

He was every burnt out cowboy
that I'd seen a million times

With dead man penny eyes,
like tarnished brass,

That reflected accusations
of his critics and his crimes

And drowned them
in the bottom of a glass.

"He's a victim," said the barkeep,
"Of a tragic circumstance.

Down deep inside him,
bad luck broke an egg.

Now his longtime compañeros
and his sagebrush confidants

All treat him like a man
who's got the plague."

He was damn sure death warmed over,
human dust upon the shelf,

Though Grasmere ain't
the center of the earth

He appeared like he'd be lonesome
at a party for himself,

So low was his opinion
of his worth.

"*Pour me two, and make'm doubles.*"
Then I slid on down the bar

And rested at the
corner of his cage.

I had judged him nearly sixty
when I saw him from afar

But eye to eye,
I'd overshot his age.

'Cause it wasn't time that changed him,
I could see that now up close,

Pure hell had cut
those tracks across his face.

His shaking hand picked up the drink,
then he gestured grandiose,

"This buys you
chapter one of my disgrace.

It was twenty years, September,
that I first laid eyes on her,

Not far from where
this story's bein' told.

She was pretty, in an awkward way,
though most would not concur,

A buckskin filly,
comin' two years old.

We were runnin' wild horses
on the Blackstone range that day.

We found'em on the flats
right after dawn.

There was me and Tom and Ziggy,
plus some guys from Diamond A.

They caught our scent
and then the race was on!

We hit'em like a hurricane
and we pressed'em to the east

A'crowdin'em
against the canyon rim

'Til the fear of God was boilin'
in the belly of the beast

And chance of their escape
was lookin' dim.

We all held the bunch together
and we matched'em stride for stride.

I took the flank
so none of them would stray.

Then I saw that buckskin filly
take a trail down the side,

I rode on by
and let her get away.

'No big deal,' I told my cronies,
  as we later reminisced

    And celebrated
    with a glass of beer,

      'She would'a made poor chicken feed,
      so I'm sorta glad I missed.

      I'll get her when we
      crack'em out next year.

*hor'enuf, next fall we found'em
up on California Crick.*

*The buckskin mare
was still amongst the pack.*

*I had made a little wager
and I aimed to make it stick,*

*Whoever roped her
pocketed the jack.*

We lined'em out and built our loops.
Then ignoring protocol,

That mare changed course
and never missed a beat!

She took dang near the entire bunch
when she climbed the canyon wall

And left us empty handed
at her feet.

*In the several years that followed
  she eluded each attempt*

*To capture her, in fact,
she seemed amused*

*And her reputation deepened,
as no doubt, did her contempt*

*For us, the bumbling cowboys
she abused.*

The legend of the buckskin mare,
which to me, was overblown,

    Was bunkhouse, barroom
    gossip everywhere.

        She achieved a kinda stature,
        way beyond mere flesh and bone,

        And stories of her deeds
        would raise your hair.

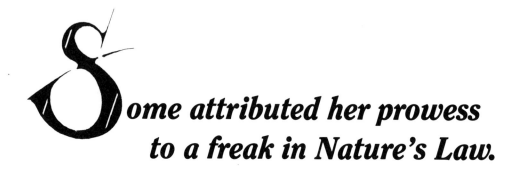

*Some attributed her prowess
to a freak in Nature's Law.*

*Still others said
she was the devil's spawn*

*So the incident that happened
at the top of Sheepshead Draw*

*Served notice hell's account
was overdrawn.*

'Cause upon that fateful gather
  there was one foolhardy dope,

  A greenhorn kid
  who didn't have a care

  But susceptible to eggin'
  and right handy with a rope

  So, 'course, we pumped him up
  about the mare.

*H*e was lathered up and tickin'
    like an ol' two dollar watch

    When we spotted
    the object of the game.

      Though we wanted other horses,
      each one ached to carve his notch

      On the buckskin mare,
      Bruneau Canyon's fame.

They were down amongst the willers
by a muddy water hole.

The kid went first.
He had her in his sights

And halfway up the other side
where the slick rock takes its toll

He caught that buckskin legend
dead to rights!

He was screamin' bloody murder
   as she clawed her way uphill!

   He pitched the slack
   and pulled his horse up hard!

      She was jerked around and faced the kid,
      and friend, if looks could kill

      I'd have folded before
      she played her card.

But the kid began descending
    with his back turned toward the mare

    He planned to choke her down,
    I won't deny,

        But she jumped from high above him,
        like a bird takes to the air,

            She looked for all the world
            like she could fly.

Time was frozen for an instant
as she leaped out into space,

A piece from some unholy carousel

And I stared, slack jawed and helpless,
in the morbid scene's embrace,

Oddly peaceful,
until the hammer fell.

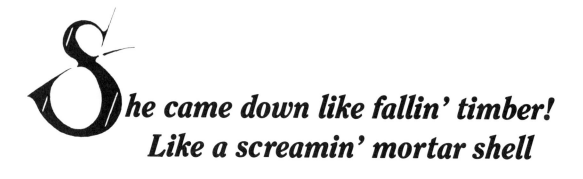

She came down like fallin' timber!
Like a screamin' mortar shell

And scattered terra firma
in her wake!

She lit runnin' off his wrong side
like a thoroughbred gazelle!

That nylon rope was hissin'
like a snake!

It flipped behind the kid's own horse.
Laid the trip as sweet as pie.

She thundered by him
takin' up the slack!

The rope drew tight around his hocks,
then she shifted into high

And jerked that horse
right over on his back!

'Course the kid fell backwards with him.
In my heart I knew his fate.

His soul was headed
for the great beyond.

She was draggin' horse and rider
like a bundle of deadweight

When Clay rode in
and cut the fatal bond.

She escaped. That goes unspoken,
toward the seeding to the west.

To our dismay
the kid had breathed his last.

She had spread his brains all over,
but ol' Maxie said it best,

'That's what ya get
fer tyin' hard and fast.'

The years creaked by like achin' joints.
Driftin' cowboys came and went.

The buckskin mare,
she held her own and stayed.

She became a constant rumor
and engendered discontent

Among the bucks
whose reps had not been made.

But to me she was an omen.
Like a black cat on the prowl.

I had no admiration
for her kind.

She began to stalk my nightmares,
an obsession loud and foul

Only drinkin'
would get her off my mind.

There were still a few ol' timers
   like Jess and Dale, Chuck and Al,

      Who spoke of her
      as one without a fault.

         They bragged her up,
         which didn't do a thing for my morale

            'Cause I'd begun to dread
            each new assault.

But I went, like I did always,
when they organized last year.

We met at Simplot's
Sheep Crick winter camp

Then headed east toward J P Point,
it was sunny, warm and clear

But I was cold.
My bones were feelin' damp.

*I*t was gettin' close to lunch time
when we finally cut their track

And found'em at the
Bruneau Canyon's verge.

We rode in like mad Apaches!
I was leadin' the attack!

The first to see us comin'
was the scourge.

The scourge of all my sleepless nights.
The bogeyman in my dreams.

I told myself,
this run would be her last.

She ducked across my horse's nose,
to draw me out, it seems.

I followed suit and
then the die was cast.

She went straight for Bruneau Canyon,
made a B-line for the edge.

My head was ringin'
with her siren's song

Then she hesitated briefly,
sorta hung there on the ledge

Like she was darin' me
to come along.

Then she wheeled, without a 'by yer leave'
and disappeared from view.

I reached the precipice
and never slowed!

I could hear the boys shoutin'
but by then I think they knew

I was rabid
and ready to explode!

We landed like an avalanche,
  my horse, a livin' landslide!

    I'll never know
    just how he kept his feet.

      My boot hooked on a buckbrush limb
      and whipped me like a riptide,

        And in the crash,
        I damn near lost my seat!

But I kept the spurs dug in him
as I held the mare in sight.

Varmints skittered,
as down the side we tore!

There were boulders big as boxcars,
Rocks who'd never lost a fight,

That stepped aside
to watch this private war.

Then the cunning crowbait got me!
  She came up to this ravine

  And jumped it!
  Looked to me like just for show.

  But I reined up hard and halted.
  There was twenty feet between

  My horse's hooves
  and sure death down below.

But no horse, no fleabag mustang,
    was a match for my resolve.

I drove the steel
in my pony's hide

'Til he leaped above the chasm!
I could feel his fear dissolve

As we sailed, soaring,
flaunting suicide!

An eternity of seconds
that concluded in a wreck

The likes of which
you've never seen before.

Nearly cleared the far embankment,
got his front feet on the deck

And pawed like someone
swimmin' for the shore!

Then he shook one final shudder
   and went limp between my knees.

      I scrambled off him,
      prayin' not to fall.

         He'd impaled himself upon a rock
         and died without a wheeze,

            His guts a'stringin'
            down the crevice wall.

*T*hen his carcass started saggin',
   slippin' off the bloody skewer.

     I lunged to save my rifle
     from the slide!

          My revenge was all that mattered,
          a disease that had no cure

               Save the stretchin'
               of one ol' buckskin's hide.

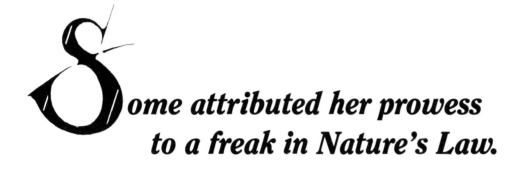

ome attributed her prowess
to a freak in Nature's Law.

Still others said
she was the devil's spawn

So the incident that happened
at the top of Sheepshead Draw

Served notice hell's account
was overdrawn.

'Cause upon that fateful gather
  there was one foolhardy dope,

    A greenhorn kid
    who didn't have a care

      But susceptible to eggin'
      and right handy with a rope

        So, 'course, we pumped him up
        about the mare.

He was lathered up and tickin'
like an ol' two dollar watch

When we spotted
the object of the game.

Though we wanted other horses,
each one ached to carve his notch

On the buckskin mare,
Bruneau Canyon's fame.

They were down amongst the willers
   by a muddy water hole.

   The kid went first.
   He had her in his sights

   And halfway up the other side
   where the slick rock takes its toll

   He caught that buckskin legend
   dead to rights!

He **was screamin' bloody murder
as she clawed her way uphill!**

**He pitched the slack
and pulled his horse up hard!**

**She was jerked around and faced the kid,
and friend, if looks could kill**

**I'd have folded before
she played her card.**

But the kid began descending
    with his back turned toward the mare

        He planned to choke her down,
        I won't deny,

            But she jumped from high above him,
            like a bird takes to the air,

                She looked for all the world
                like she could fly.

*Time was frozen for an instant
as she leaped out into space,*

A piece from some unholy carousel

*And I stared, slack jawed and helpless,
in the morbid scene's embrace,*

*Oddly peaceful,
until the hammer fell.*

*S*he came down like fallin' timber!
Like a screamin' mortar shell

And scattered terra firma
in her wake!

She lit runnin' off his wrong side
like a thoroughbred gazelle!

That nylon rope was hissin'
like a snake!

79/54